RHYTHM&NOTATION
FORDRUMS

The Complete Guide to Rhythm Reading & Reading Drum Music

KEV O'SHEA

FUNDAMENTALCHANGES

Rhythm & Notation For Drums

The Complete Guide to Rhythm Reading & Reading Drum Music

ISBN: 978-1-911267-54-6

Published by **www.fundamental-changes.com**

www.fundamental-changes.com

Twitter: @guitar_joseph

Over 10,000 fans on Facebook: **FundamentalChangesInGuitar**

Instagram: **FundamentalChanges**

For over 350 Free Guitar Lessons with Videos Check Out

www.fundamental-changes.com

Cover Image Copyright: Shutterstock Oleksandr Nagaiets

Contents

Get the Audio

The audio files for this book are available to download for free from www.fundamental-changes.com. The link is in the top right-hand corner. Simply select this book title from the drop-down menu and follow the instructions to get the audio.

We recommend that you download the files directly to your computer, not to your tablet, and extract them there before adding them to your media library. You can then put them on your tablet, iPod or burn them to CD. On the download page there is a help PDF and we also provide technical support via the contact form.

For over 350 Free Lessons with Videos Check out:

www.fundamental-changes.com

Over 10,000 fans on Facebook: **FundamentalChangesInGuitar**

Instagram: **FundamentalChanges**

Part One: Notation and Rhythmic Value

Introduction

Many musicians learn to play an instrument without any knowledge of the fundamentals of reading music. Indeed, while learning to read music is not essential, there are many distinct advantages. For example, complex concepts can be expressed and understood without the need to play or listen. The knowledge of written music is another important communication device.

This book covers the essential points you need to know when reading rhythm on the drum set. As drummers, rhythm is all important and once you have a steady grasp of the basic note values, everything else will come naturally.

Music for all instruments is written on a staff (or stave):

The staff is where we place the drum notation and it consists of five straight lines. At the beginning of this staff you will notice a " || " symbol. This is a drum or percussion *clef*. Clefs indicate what instrument or key a piece of music is written in, but in drum notation sometime no clef is used.

Notes can be placed *on* the lines, *in between* the lines or even *above and below* the staff.

Each line or space represents an individual drum.

On the following page is an example of a *drum key*. This drum key shows common examples of where we place drums when writing.

Different drum books often use different drum keys. Don't fret over minor differences as normally everything becomes clear with context and experience.

Drum Key

The symbols used for notating drums and cymbals can vary from one piece of music to another. Here is one example of a guide to reading the staff:

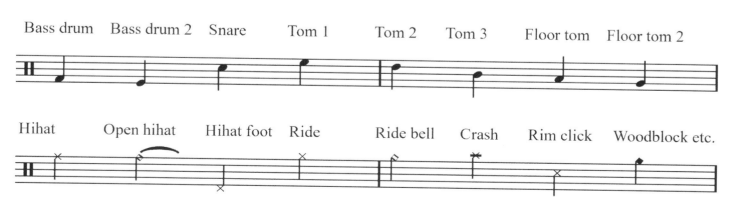

Note Key

The following examples show different length note-heads. A note can be anywhere from the length of a bar to a fraction of a beat. These examples are in the time signature '4/4' which means there are four, 1/4 note beats in each bar. We will examine time signatures in much more detail later.

Each example is split into two bars. The first bar shows each note value and the second bar shows the equivalent 'rest' value. Rests simply indicate silence, or when *not* to play.

A whole note (sometimes called a semibreve) followed by a whole note rest:

Two half notes (minims) followed by two half note rests:

1/4 notes (crotchets) followed by 1/4 note rests:

1/8th notes (quavers) followed by 1/8th note rests and 1/4 note rests:

This example shows 1/16th notes (semiquavers) and their respective rests:

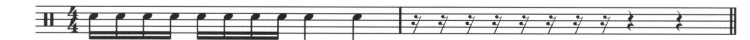

1/32nd notes (demisemiquavers) and rests:

1/64th notes (hemidemisemiquavers) and rests:

Music notation is mathematical in nature. A whole note is twice the length of a half note. A half note is twice the length of a 1/4 note. This pattern continues, giving us a range of smaller units with different note values.

It is these note values that help us define music in the written form.

For every note value, there is an equivalent *rest* value. Rests are used to indicate the periods of silence in music.

Before we move on, examine each note and its corresponding rest. Become familiar with them and their differences. You will notice the 1/8th note is made up of a solid black head, stem and tail. The corresponding picture shows two 1/8th notes joined together by their tails. The 1/8th note rest also has one tail and looks like a number '7'.

As you examine the 1/16th notes, 1/32nd notes and 1/64th notes, you can see how extra tails are added to indicate note value. These tails are crucial to understanding note length in musical notation.

Each note has an alternative name in parentheses, such as crotchet or quaver. These are the traditional names for the note and are commonly used in classical music terminology.

Although it is helpful to know both sets of names, in this book I will mainly use the fractional terms such as 1/8th, 1/16th, 1/32nd, etc., as this makes explaining time signatures much easier.

Time Signatures

The time signature is one of the most important considerations when reading music. Time signatures are pronounced as they are written, so:

3/4 is "three, four"

9/8 is "nine, eight"

21/16 is "twenty-one, sixteen"

The number on the bottom refers to the type of beat to be counted. The number on the top refers to the how many of these beats there are per bar.

Let's take **4/4** as an example. The top number tells us there are four beats in the bar. The bottom number tells us each beat is a '1/4 note' or a 'crotchet'.

This 1/4 note usually refers to the metronome bpm (beats per minute) settings we see on sheets of music. The 1/4 note is the 'pulse' of a song. It is the reference to which every other note value relates.

A bpm setting of 60 means '60 **B**eats **P**er **M**inute' – one beat every second. Let us examine the mathematics involved with note values.

Every 1/4 note is equal in length to two 1/8th notes (also called quavers):

Notice that in the first bar the 1/4 note is followed by three 1/4 note rests. In the second bar the two 1/8th notes are followed by a 1/4 note rest *and* a half note rest.

Each 1/8th note is represented by a note head, a stem and *one* tail. In the above example the two 1/8th note tails are joined together.

Never join an 1/8th note tail to a 1/4 note otherwise it will make the 1/4 look like an 1/8th note.

If the 1/4 note (at 60 bpm) is played once every second, then the 1/8th notes will be played at the rate of *twice* every second.

1/4 note = played every 1 second

1/8th note = played every half second

Try this yourself. Tap along to a metronome set at 60 bpm, or if you don't have a metronome, use the second hand on a clock as a reference. The second hand naturally ticks 60 times a minute.

Fig. 1

Tapping once every second defines the 1/4 note at 60 bpm. By doubling the speed of the tap, we create 1/8th notes.

Fig. 2

The 1/4 note is also equal in length to four 1/16th notes (semiquavers):

Fig. 3

Each 1/16th note is represented by a note head, a stem and *two* tails. When 1/16th notes are played consecutively these tails are also joined together. Normally, when you have a long sequence of 1/16th notes they are separated into groups of four. This both makes it easier to read, and establishes where the 1/4 note pulse is.

As with 1/8th notes, you must never join a 1/16th note tail to a 1/4 note. Having a tail changes the value of the 1/4 note.

You can, however, join 1/16th notes and 1/8th notes:

Fig. 4

Notice how each 1/8th note is joined to two 1/16th notes with a tail. This convention is extremely important when we read music. The clue to the note's value is always in the tail(s), or lack thereof.

If a 1/4 note (at 60 bpm) is counted once every second, and the 1/8th notes are twice every second, then 1/16th notes will be at the rate of *four* every second.

Therefore at 60 bpm:

1/4 note = played every 1 second

1/8th note = played every .5 seconds

1/16th notes = played every .25 seconds

Snare Exercise

Set your metronome to 60 bpm. This is the 1/4 note pulse.

Count out loud as you play each beat on your snare (or table top!). Listen to the audio example to hear how this should sound.

Example 1a

Next, play 1/8th notes. This rhythm is twice the speed of the last example. For every 60bpm pulse we will now play *two* notes.

Count this phrase out loud as you play each 1/8th note:

Example 1b

The 60-bpm pulse is indicated by each number (1, 2, 3, and 4). Lock into to the metronome with your counting.

It is important that the 1/8th note count splits each 1/4 note count precisely in two so that the 1/8th notes are played exactly double the speed of the 1/4 notes.

Combinations

Next, we will look at combining 1/4 notes with 1/8th notes. With your metronome set to 60 bpm, count along with the piece:

Example 1c

Each number count should land on the metronome click. The additional 1/8th (the 'and') should land *exactly* between beats 3 and 4.

Notice how the added 1/8th note does *not* join to the 1/4 note on beat 4. 1/4 notes must never be joined with tails.

Now a syncopated (off-beat) example that introduces 1/8th note rests:

Example 1d

The 'C' at the beginning of the notation is short for *common time*, another way of writing **4/4**.

We could use 1/4 notes to notate the same rhythm:

Remember, 1/4 notes are equal in length to two 1/8th notes. This means there are the same number of notes in this example as the previous one. The notes are played with identical timing to the last example. The only difference is the *length* of the notes.

As drummers, the *length* of a note is not usually a concern because drum sounds do not have much *sustain*.

Next, we will use off-beats exclusively. Each note falls on an 'and' between the 1 2 3 4 count:

Example 1e

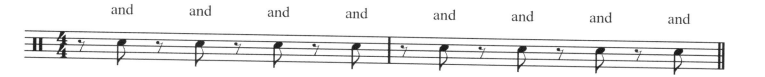

Each hit here lands exactly between the metronome pulse. Count out loud to help you time each note.

1/16th Notes

Next, we will play 1/16th notes. This rhythm is double the speed of 1/8th notes. That's four notes per 60 bpm pulse.

Count "1 e and a 2 e and a 3 e and a 4 e and a" out loud as you play each 1/16th note:

Example 1f

There are now four divisions to represent each 1/16th note: '1', 'e', 'and', 'a'.

Lock in with the metronome by counting steadily out loud.

It is important that the 1/16th note count splits each 1/4 note count exactly into *four*. The 1/16th notes are exactly *twice* the speed of the 1/8th notes.

Next, an example containing 1/8th notes and 1/16th notes. Again, count aloud along to the metronome:

Example 1g

Examine beat 2. It is made up of one 1/8th note and two 1/16th notes. Usually, a group of four consecutive 1/16th notes is counted:

"1 e and a"

or

"2 e and a" etc.

In this example, there is no need to count the second 1/16th note – the "e". The 1/8th note lasts for the duration of the first two 1/16th notes ("2 e"), giving us:

"2 and a"

With an example like this, you can count the "e" *silently:*

Example 1h

It is important to be able to recognise the different combinations of 1/8th notes and 1/16th notes and how they are counted.

With the metronome at 60 bpm tap along with the next few examples:

Example 1i

Example 1j

Example 1k

Example 1l

Example 1m

In the next example, we avoid playing any 'down' beats (1, 2, 3 and 4). Count each beat out loud while tapping the notated rhythm.

Example 1n

Dotted Notes

Examine the following 1/4 note and observe the small dot placed after the note head:

The instruction the dot gives us it to *increase the value of the written note by half.*

One 1/4 note has the same duration of two 1/8th notes so one *dotted 1/4 note* equals the length of *three* 1/8th notes.

Dotted Notes vs. Rests

Because drummers usually need not worry about the length of any given note, we can notate music in many ways. We can use *long notes* or *short notes with rests*.

For example, this can be counted:

Example 1o

The first note is a dotted 1/4 note, so it lasts for the length of three 1/8th notes.

Sometimes dotted notes are used in drum notation. Other times they can be replaced by rests.

Look at the following example which uses two 1/8th note rests and plays a similar pattern:

For a drummer, there is no difference in playing either of the previous two examples. This is because sustain (length of note) is not often a concern when drumming.

This next example is again identical for drummers:

The bar starts with a 1/4 note plus an 1/8th note rest. This again equals three 1/8th notes, or one dotted 1/4 note.

Dotted 1/8th notes

Let's look at dotted 1/8th notes. By adding half of the value, the *dotted 1/8th note* becomes equal to the length of *three 1/16th notes* (1/8th note + 1/16th note).

In the following example notice how the first note (a dotted 1/8th) is followed by a 1/16th note rest. The dotted 1/8th note equals the value of three 1/16th notes and the following rest completes beat 1.

Beat 2 is a 1/4 note rest. Beat 3 is one 1/16th note followed by three 1/16th note rests. Finally beat 4 shows a 1/4 note rest.

On drums, a dotted 1/8th note sounds the same as a 1/16th note followed by an 1/8th note rest. Both have the value of three 1/16th notes.

Because note length does not play a big part in basic drum kit notation, we can use rests whenever they are convenient. Quite often a decision to use rests is based on the keeping appearance of the written music tidy and clear. Too many rests can leave a drum part cluttered and confusing.

However, cymbals can sustain for a long time, so if you see a rest after a cymbal hit you should ensure you only allow it to ring for the set period.

Introducing Drum Beats

Let's use what we know to learn how a basic rock drum beat builds around a 4/4, 60bpm pulse. Each bar contains four 1/4 note beats. First, we add the bass drum and the snare:

Count out loud and play the following ideas.

Example 1p

The first count is on the bass drum and the second is on the snare. This pattern repeats on beats 3 and 4.

Note stems may point upwards or downwards, depending on convenience. In most cases drum notation will point upwards to tie in with the hi-hats/cymbals at the top of the staff.

Add an extra bass drum to the "and" of beat 3. Count along:

Example 1q

Next add the hi-hat. The hi-hat plays 1/8th notes. Pay careful attention to how the tails on the 1/8th note tie together.

The 1/8th note hi-hats are counted as follows:

Example 1r

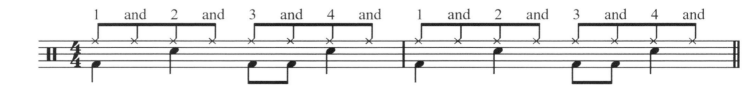

Verbally accent the pulse on beats 1, 2, 3 and 4 while counting the 1/8th notes in between.

This rhythm can be notated in different ways. For example, you can place all tails in an upward direction so that they tie together above the staff:

In the above example, each bass drum and snare hit has been written as an 1/8th note and all now have one tail. From a drummer's perspective, there is no difference in how the two examples above are played.

Next, we will switch to playing 1/16th notes on the hi-hat. Each 1/16th note contains *two tails* that tie together. Remember, there are four 1/16th notes in every 1/4 note beat.

We count 1/16th notes as:

1 e and a 2 e and a 3 e and a 4 e and a   etc.

Now place these 1/16th notes into the drum beat.

Pay careful attention to where the bass drum and snare should land:

Example 1s

1 e and a 2 e and a 3 e and a 4 e and a   etc.

Now let's try some combinations that involve syncopation (off beat playing) between the bass drum and hi-hat:

Example 1t

1 and a 2 and 3 and 4 and   1 and a 2 and 3 and 4 and

We could notate the cymbals both above or below and the drums:

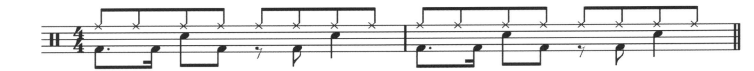

The hi-hat plays a simple pattern on each 1/8th note:

"<u>1</u> and <u>2</u> and <u>3</u> and <u>4</u> and"

The bass drum and snare are a bit trickier. In this example, they are notated separately from the hi-hat. The bass drum plays the following <u>underlined</u> counts:

"<u>1</u> e and <u>**a**</u> 2 e <u>**and**</u> a 3 e <u>**and**</u> a 4 e and a"

The snare plays only on '2' and '4':

"1 e and a <u>2</u> e and a 3 e and a <u>4</u> e and a"

Both are legitimate ways of interpreting the beat.

Mid Bar Line

When we write drum notation in 4/4 it is good practice to avoid joining beat 2 to beat 3. This makes it easier to read complex pieces. The rule is to always show the gap between beat 2 and beat 3 when playing in 4/4.

Here is an example of a poorly written drum score:

The 1/8th note groupings are divided into groups of three, three and two. The second grouping starts on the fourth hi-hat. This count is the 'and' of beat 2. The 1/8th note joins beat 3 – a rookie mistake.

The mid-point of a 4/4 bar, is beat 3. Beat 3 should *never* be joined from the previous beat.

This is how the above rhythm should be notated:

The bar is divided cleanly in half. Making the mid-point of the bar obvious makes reading music easier.

In **4/4**, you can join beat **1** to beat **2,** and beat **3** to beat **4**, but never beat **2** to beat **3**.

Ties

When you see a symbol above or below a note head like this:

It's telling the musician to 'tie' one note into the next. In other words, hold the first note for the length of the two notes together.

You may have noticed a **%** symbol in the second bar. This symbol means "repeat the previous bar".

Ties are important for sustaining instruments, such as guitar or trumpet, but for a drummer they often have little relevance. That said, it is important to know how to read ties, as many instructional books still use them.

Playing this bar on the snare drum:

Example 1u

Is the equivalent to playing:

The tie in the first example is on the 'a' of beat 3. It ties to the first note of beat 4. On a pitched instrument this would be a signal to hold the note for the length of two 1/16th notes. In drumming terms, we simply play the tied second note as a rest.

So why bother learning about ties in the first place? Well, imagine you are reading the melody of a song and you need to accent each note in a certain passage. This technique is very common, especially in jazz.

Many melodies contain ties, and sometimes they even extend from one bar to the next. In certain cases, you might find multiple ties as shown below:

In this case, only the *first* note of the tied group is played (the 'and' of beat 4). It is held until the end of the second note in bar two.

Many snare and stick control books use ties, so become familiar with them.

Now let's revise everything we have covered in Part One.

Revision 1

Play through the following rhythm exercise. You can play this on a table top, a snare drum, or even different drums on your kit.

At 60 bpm play using one hand

At 120 bpm play using both two hands alternating

Example 1v

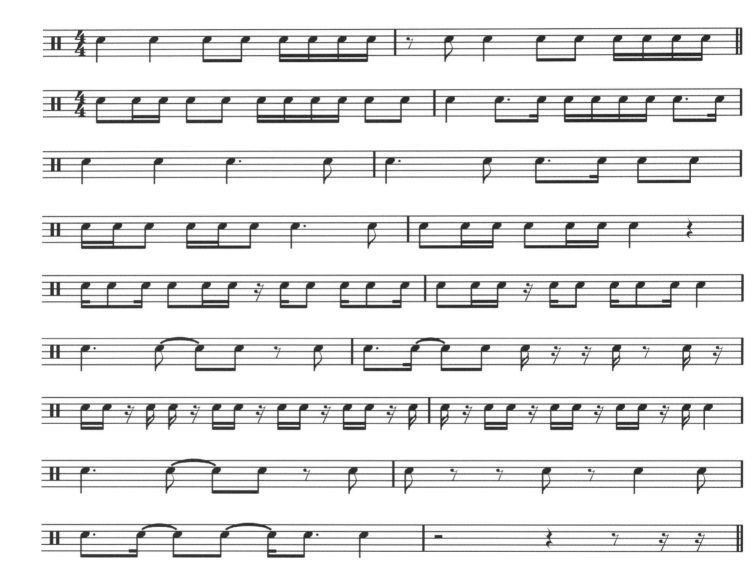

Part Two: Complex Time Signatures

3/4

We have looked at basic rock beats in **4/4**. Now we will examine some more complex time signatures.

3/4 is an oft-used time signature. It literally reads as "three 1/4 notes beats per bar".

That may seem confusing; three 1/4s?! Where's the other 1/4?

Remember, music notation goes back many hundreds of years. If we were to re-define the rules nowadays we would quite possibly use different terminology.

Despite being called a 1/4 note now, the real (English) name for a 1/4 note is a *crotchet*. While the name "1/4 note" relates to a specific division of a bar, the name crotchet does not. So, we *can* have three, four or five crochets in a bar without getting confused by the math! When you see 3/4 or 5/4, *think* three crotchets or five crotchets (or beats) in a bar. Try *not* to think of three 1/4 notes or five 1/4 notes in a bar.

Treat the 1/4 note merely as a term for the 'pulse' and not as a strict form of mathematical division. 3/4 means we will have three pulses, or 'beats', per bar.

Here is an example of a 3/4 rock beat:

Example 2a

Notice how each set of tail-groupings outlines each of the three beats in the bar.

9/8

9/8 is an interesting time signature and can help explain some of the anomalies encountered in music reading.

As you can guess, **9/8** refers to there being nine 1/8th notes in a bar. These 1/8th notes will now become the count, just like the 1/4 notes were the count in earlier examples.

"1, 2, 3, 4, 5, 6, 7, 8, 9"

In this example, it may seem like there is no difference between **9/8** and **9/4**, and to a certain extent that's true. The difference with **9/8** is that there is flexibility in how we group the 1/8th notes.

For example, **9/8** is *normally* as three groups of 3:

*"**1**, 2, 3, **4**, 5, 6, **7**, 8, 9"*

I have underlined the emphasised counts and made them **bold**. Time signatures that are grouped in threes in this way are commonly referred to as *compound* time signatures.

Here is how a compound **9/8** beat might be notated:

Example 2b

Placing the tails down in this manner is optional. Notice how the last snare is a dotted 1/4 note. This lasts for a count of three 1/8th notes (7, 8 & 9).

Grouping the 1/8th notes into threes makes them easier to read for the musician and dictates the intended feel.

Bpm indicators may use the 1/8th note or a dotted 1/4 notes to show you how to count the pulse.

The following bpm indicators show the same tempo because the length of **three** 1/8th notes is equal to **one** dotted 1/4 note.

To feel this in action, set your metronome to 180 bpm. It will play three clicks every second. The metronome click now represents the pulse – in this case, the 1/8th note. Now try setting the metronome to 60 and counting three notes per click. You are now counting the 1/8th notes while the metronome clicks the dotted 1/4 note beat.

Let's introduce some 1/16th notes to the **9/8** beat:

Example 2c

Every 1/8th note is the value of two 1/16th notes. In this case we count groups of 1/16th notes as "*1 a*" or "*1 and*", etc.

9/8 could also be counted as:

Example 2d

This looks just like a rock beat in **4/4** but with an added 1/8th note at the end. Instead of being grouped in threes, the 1/8th notes are now a mix of two and three-note groupings.

As you can see, the snare and bass drum pattern consists of three 1/4 notes and one dotted 1/4 note.

Three 1/4 notes (six 1/8th notes)

+

One dotted 1/4 note (three 1/8th notes)

=

nine 1/8th notes (9/8)

When you see a time signature with an '8' at the bottom, it most often means the groupings will be divided into a triplet feel (groups of three). If you see a '4' at the bottom, the groupings will most often be even.

9/8 most commonly sounds like three groups of three. 12/8 most commonly sounds like four groups of three.

Additive Time Signatures

Additive time signatures are sometimes used if further clarity is needed in a piece of music. The following example of an additive time signature shows us how **8/8** could be notated:

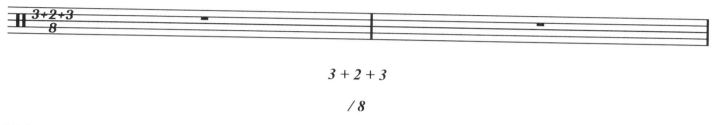

$$3 + 2 + 3$$

$$/ 8$$

8/8 is a rare time signature and equal in duration to **4/4**. Writing the signature as 8/8 allows us to see how the composer wishes us to feel the beat divisions.

Often, when you see a time signature like **9/8** or **7/8** the feel is not immediately clear. You must look at how the notes are grouped to see how the pulse is intended to be played. In certain cases, the feel might even change from bar to bar.

Here is are examples of two different **7/8** feels:

Example 2e

Example 2f

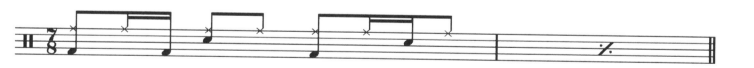

In the first example, **7/8** is divided into groups of 3, 2 and 2.

In the second example, **7/8** is divided into groups of 2, 2 and 3.

7/8 and other 'odd' time signatures such as **5/4** are sometimes referred to as *complex* time signatures.

Time signatures give us a basic framework in which to play. Concepts like 'feel' are made evident by the groupings of the notes themselves which is why additive time signatures are useful.

Time Signatures Greater than /16

Time signatures involving /16 are usually more complex than /8 or /4.

13/16, for example, can be divided in many ways. Here is an example of a beat in 13/16:

Example 2g

The beat is divided into groups of 4, 4 and 5.

Here is another example where groups of 3 are used:

Example 2h

This beat is divided into groups of 3, 3, 3 and 4.

Time Signatures Greater than /4

Time signatures using notes longer than 1/4 notes are less common in modern music but the same principles apply.

3/2 tells us the bar is made up of three *half notes*. Half notes are equal to *twice* the length of 1/4 notes.

Three half notes = six 1/4 notes. By that logic, a bar of **3/2** is equal in length to a bar of **6/4**.

'1' can also be used in time signatures, as in **3/1**. This shows that bar is made up of three *whole notes*.

One whole note is equal to four 1/4 notes, so this bar would equal the length of twelve 1/4 notes, or **12/4**.

Mixed Metres

On rare occasions, a time signature is written as two 'mixed' metres.

Example 2i

The first bar is compound time and is divided into groups of three 1/8th notes. The second bar is in **5/4** with an emphasis on the 1/4 note (every two 1/8th notes).

This is a convenient way of telling the performer how to perform a complex piece. Placing the signatures at the beginning of the bars means the reader knows what to expect. The technique of using two recurring time signatures can, in theory continue every two bars, until otherwise indicated.

Don't obsess over these rare cases. As a drummer, 99% of the time signatures you will encounter will be either be **/4**, **/8** or, very occasionally, **/16**.

1/32nd Notes (Demisemiquavers)

Reading 1/32nd notes is much like reading 1/16th notes. To develop a greater sense of 1/32nd notes play the following exercise.

Set your metronome to 60 bpm and play the following pattern with one hand:

You are playing 1/16th notes at 60 bpm. Precisely four taps a second.

Now introduce your other hand to create a single stroke roll:

Example 2j

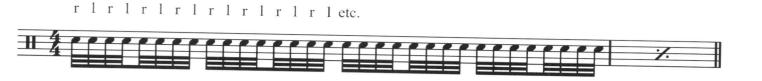

You should now be playing eight individual notes for every metronome click.

These are 1/32nd notes at 60 bpm.

Therefore at 60 bpm:

1/4 note = one note every 1 second

1/8th note = one note every .5 seconds

1/16th notes = one note every .25 seconds

1/32nd notes = *one note every .125 seconds* – *8 times a second*

As shown in the Note Key in **Part One**, 1/32nd notes have three tails. You can see the relationship between 1/32nd notes and 1/16th notes below:

Example 2k

Here is a drum beat with 1/32nd notes on the hi-hat.

Example 2l

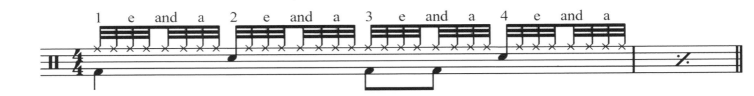

Pay careful attention to how the count relates to the 1/32nd note groupings.

Next, alternate between 1/32nds and 1/16th notes on the hi-hat:

Example 2m

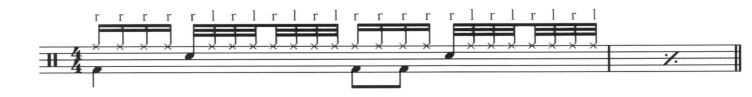

Here we can use the leading hand ('r' in this case) to play the 1/16th notes and fill in the 1/32nd notes with the other hand. Stay in time to the metronome on each beat.

Example 2n

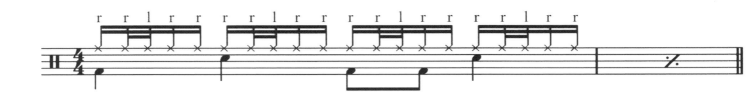

Notice how the 1/32nd note and 1/16th note tails relate to each other:

Example 2o

The note values above in beat 1 are: 1/32nd, 1/32nd, 1/16th, 1/32nd, 1/32nd, 1/16th. These add up to one 1/4 note.

Example 2p

The above note values for beat 1 are: 1/16th, 1/32nd, 1/32nd, 1/16th, 1/32nd, 1/32nd.

Example 2q

The above note values for beat 1 are: 1/32nd, 1/16th, 1/32nd, 1/32nd, 1/16th, 1/32nd (one 1/4 note).

Notice how only **two** tails from the 1/32nd note connect to the 1/16th note.

In the following example, we will use rests to show the difference between 1/16ths and 1/32nds.

1/16th note rests are equal in length to two 1/32nd note rests.

Example 2r

Listen to the audio example. You can hear that the same rhythm is effectively notated on both beats 1 and 2.

1/64th Notes and Beyond...

There is a logical progression between the number of tails a note has and the length of the note.

1/64th notes (hemidemisemiquavers) are exactly half the length of 1/32nd notes. Each note is represented by *four* tails.

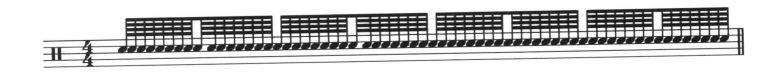

Therefore at 60 bpm:

1/4 note = one note every 1 second

1/8th note = one note every .5 seconds

1/16th notes = one note every .25 seconds

1/32nd notes = one note every .125 seconds

1/64th notes = *one note every .0625 seconds – 16 times a second*

1/64th notes are rare in drum notation. Focus on becoming familiar with 1/4 notes, 1/8th notes and 1/16ths. In time 1/32nd notes will become easier to read.

There are smaller divisions like 1/124th notes (5 tails, but these are extremely rare. The chances are you will never encounter a piece of music with divisions smaller than 1/64th notes).

Longer than 1/4s

Notes longer than 1/4 notes are not common in most drum notation. Because we play an instrument where long sustained notes are rare, we need not use note heads longer than a 1/4 note.

It is, however, important to learn the value of all the **rests** bigger than 1/4 notes.

For example, a dotted 1/4 note rest (the length of three 1/8th notes):

A half note rest (the length of two 1/4 note rests):

On beat 4, you will notice a dotted 1/8th note rest followed by a whole note rest in bar two.

Shuffle and Swing

Shuffle is a feel many drummers are familiar with. Here is an example of a basic shuffle beat.

Example 2s

The time signature here is **12/8**. We will treat this as a compound time signature and divide the 1/8th notes into groups of three.

We play a 1/4 note + 1/8th note for the hi-hat pattern (four times). If you count the values, you will find that they all add up to **twelve** 1/8th notes.

The bass drum and snare are made up of four dotted 1/4 notes, again adding up to twelve 1/8th notes.

A shuffle could also be counted in this way:

Each dotted 1/4 can be treated as a pulse and counted. For example, a piece of music might contain directions such as:

Indicating a tempo of *three* 1/8th notes per second.

Shuffles can also be notated in **4/4** like this:

Example 2t

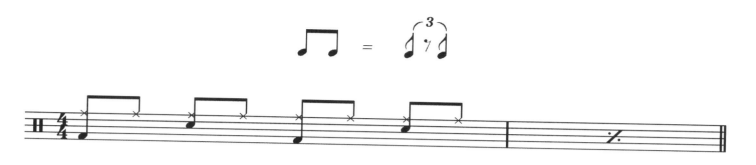

The above notation looks just like a straight rock 4/4 beat but the instruction above the stave tells us to swing the 1/8th notes. As you can hear in *audio example 2t*, the feel is a shuffle, much like the previous example in 12/8.

The instruction is to treat each group of 1/8th notes in a triplet fashion. Notice how this group of 1/8th notes has a small '3' above. This is what indicates the 1/8ths are to be played with a triplet feel.

Also, there is an 1/8th note rest in between the triplet grouping. This means you should play the 1/8th notes as if they were the *first* and *last* 1/8ths of a triplet, resting on the second.

Shuffles are closely related to swing. Here is a basic jazz ride pattern notated in **12/8**:

Example 2u

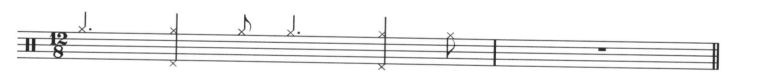

And here it is written in the more common **4/4**:

Example 2v

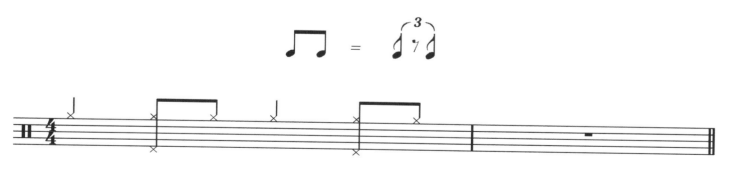

As you may have noticed, jazz swing is traditionally notated in **/4** instead of **/8**.

In early American music, many pieces were written in **3/4** or **4/4**, These were common time signatures in classical music and often used to write many of the jazz standards of the day.

Here is an example of a standard looking melody written in **4/4**:

This melody may have been written for a pitched instrument but to drummers the rhythm looks straightforward.

To create a different feel, performers would often *swing* the 1/8th notes. 'Straight' 1/8th notes were instead played in a triplet fashion.

When we play with swing, the first 1/8th note is slightly longer than usual and the second 1/8th note is slightly shorter than usual.

This means the second swung 1/8th note is played a fraction later than when played 'straight'. In conceptual terms, the second 1/8th note changes in length from half a beat to one-third of a beat.

Swing feel divides the 1/4 note *unevenly* using triplets as the basis. Although this explains swing in a technical sense *it is not an exact science*. Every person has their own inherent sense of swing and this individuality should be encouraged.

As drum parts were documented over time, the swing pattern was depicted in instructional books as 1/16th notes...

Example 2w

The above example shows the swing pattern notated as a dotted 1/8th note plus one 1/16th note. Here, swing is represented by the first and last notes of a group of **four** 1/16ths.

Nowadays it is more common to write swing as it relates to triplets.

Example 2x

We can also apply the same technique to 1/16th notes:

Example 2y

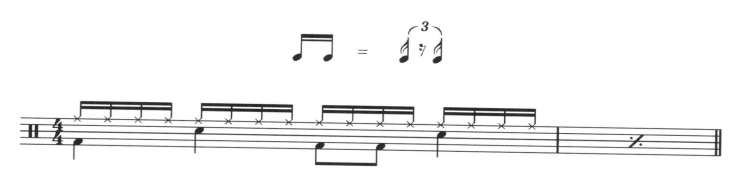

Every two 1/16th notes are to be played with a swing feel, just like the 1/8th notes in earlier examples. Have a listen to the audio example for reference.

Let's revise the concepts you've learnt in Part Two.

Revision 2

Example 2z

80 Bpm (8th note = 160 Bpm)

Straight 8th note feel...

Swing 8ths...

Straight 16ths...

Swing 16ths...

Part Three: Tips and Terminology

Tuplets

In this final section, we will cover the other terms and symbols you will encounter in notated drum music. At the end of this chapter we will discuss some techniques for writing your own notation.

Tuplets are any number of notes grouped together. They are shown by a corresponding number placed above the grouping.

3 = triplet

A triplet is a type of tuplet. In the following example, beat 3 and 4 are now grouped as 1/8th note triplets instead of regular 1/8th notes. The same rules apply to tuplet rests.

Example 3a

And now with added rests…

Example 3b

Next, the final beat is a group of three even notes. These are often referred to as '1/8th note triplets'.

Example 3c

In compound time, a group of three 1/8th notes can be substituted for four even notes.

Example 3d

4 = *quadruplet*

Practise this example to a metronome to become familiar with the difference in feel.

In the following example, five 1/16ths replaces a group of four 1/16ths. First get comfortable with the sound of five groupings at a low tempo. Then increase the tempo, while switching between regular 1/16ths. Quintuplets are covered in greater detail in my book 'Filling Time'.

Example 3e

5 = *quintuplet*

The final beat substitutes a standard group of four 1/16ths for a group of six even notes. Notice how this example is made up of both 1/16th notes and 1/8th notes – all adding up to six 1/16th notes.

Example 3f

6 = *sextuplet*

The sextuplet is like the earlier triplet example. In the earlier example, groups of 3 replaced groups of 2. In this example, groups of 6 replace groups of 4. 1/16th notes grouped like this over a 1/4 note are commonly referred to as '1/16th note triplets'.

Septuplets are rare but it is helpful to know that the same principles apply. Here seven beats occupy the same time space as a regular 1/4 note beat.

Example 3g

7 = *septuplet*

You can encounter tuplets with bigger groups of numbers. The important thing to recognise is *how many beats the tuplet grouping spans.*

The above examples all are to be played over **one** beat – A 1/4 note, or in compound time, a dotted 1/4.

This technique can also be used over other note values. Here is an example using '1/4 note triplets':

Example 3h

The above triplet grouping spans *two* beats – beats **3** and **4.**

At 60 bpm:

Each 1/4 note is the length of 1 second

Each half note is the length of 2 seconds

*Each 1/4 note triplet is the length of .6666 seconds (1 third of **2** seconds)*

In some cases, tuplets can cross the mid-bar line.

Example 3i

Tuplet Rests

The same rules apply when using rests in groups of tuplets. Here is an example involving quintuplets.

The 1/16th note rest marks the third quintuplet:

Example 3j

The 1/8th note rest represents the second and third quintuplet:

Example 3j (same rhythm)

The 1/4 note rest below instructs us to rest for the first four quintuplets, then play the fifth. This is quite a complex example and shown only to illustrate the mechanics of using rests within tuplet groupings:

Example 3k

Open Hi-Hat Symbols

Open hi-hats can be notated in several ways. One common way is to use an 'O' above the notated hi-hat symbol. This is sometimes accompanied by a short stroke that resembles a tie. The instruction is to play the open hi-hat for the length of the stroke. In other cases, the 'X' is simply replaced with 'O' to indicate an opened hi-hat.

You may sometimes see an additional hi-hat pedal symbol below the stave to indicate when to close the hi-hat.

Example 3l

Ghost Notes

A *ghost note* is a term given to playing very lightly on a drum. The aim is to play a note that is barely perceptible in comparison to a regular stroke. In most cases this applies to the snare drum, given its wide range of dynamic possibilities.

Here is a beat containing ghost notes on the snare. They are notated by placing parenthesis - '( )' - around the note head.

Example 3m

Half time

Terms like *pulse* are quite subjective. The *pulse* generally refers to where you might tap your foot.

Take this example:

Example 3n

And now in halftime:

Example 3o

The difference is obvious. While there is some similarity in how the beat is organised, the *count* is different. Counting to a metronome will highlight the difference in the previous examples.

We are quite familiar with playing the back-beat snare on 2 and 4 in a standard **4/4** beat.

In this halftime example, the snare instead lands on beat 3. This is a pretty common technique and is used quite a lot in pop songs, particularly in Dubstep, to change the feel. It can sound like the pulse changes from every 1/4 note to every half note.

Halftime is a term that applies to drums much more than any other instrument.

Flams

Flams are the drumming equivalent to adding a 'grace' note to a stroke. We take a regular stroke and precede it with a note of lower volume.

This example shows a right-handed stroke on the snare *preceded* by a left-handed grace note. This gives us a *right-handed flam*:

Example 3p

Flams should sound like *one enhanced stroke* rather than two rhythmically separate notes.

Drags

Drags are two notes together. Often, they are played as a double stroke. Here is an example of a drag used in a beat context:

Example 3q

The two left-hand strokes are played just before the following passage of 1/16th notes to create a grace note feel of a lower volume. This is a way of phrasing the drag so that it broadens the following note - similar to the way a flam does.

Drags are sometimes to be played with a defined rhythmic value – in this case 1/32nd notes. The following pattern is notated in such a manner.

Example 3r

You may also hear drags referred to as 'ruffs'.

Three-Note Drags

Three note drags are exactly that. In some cases, sticking will be provided. If no sticking is provided you can use your own variations. Again, this technique is sometimes called a 'ruff'.

Rudimental Notation

For convenience, short hand is often used, specifically when working with rudiments.

The following diagrams show two ways of notating the same pattern.

1)

2)

Examine the last bar of the first example. It contains a dotted 1/4 note tied into an 1/8th note on the 'and' of beat 2. This 1/4 note also has *two* lines through it – similar to the two tails on a 1/16th note. This tells us to play 1/16th notes for the duration of a dotted 1/4, then end on an 1/8th note. Start with the right hand and end on the left hand.

This roll becomes a total of seven strokes. If you are familiar with rudiments you will know of the *7-stroke roll* – a series of three double strokes followed by an accented single stroke.

You can play the 7-stroke roll both 'open' and 'closed'. 'Open' is when we play clean audible strokes, as in the above 1/16th note example.

'Closed' is when we play each double stroke as a press roll. A press/buzz roll is a multiple bounce roll created by carefully pressing the stick into the head to create many fast notes for each stroke.

Notation like this is used heavily in rudimental drumming as it can make a busy piece much easier to read at a glance. You may also encounter it in drum kit notation too.

Double-dotted Notes

You'll be pleased to know Double-dotted notes are not commonly found in drum notation!

As you know, a dot adds on half the original note value. A double dot adds on an additional quarter of the original note value.

Here's an example using a double-dotted 1/4 note.

First, add half the original note value (+ 1/8th note)

Then, add 1/4 the original note value (+ 1/16th note)

The resulting note is the length of *seven* 1/16th notes:

Example 3s

It is more common to notate double-dotted rhythms with ties.

Slurs vs Ties

In the first bar we see a slur from one note to another. The second bar shows a tie.

Slurs are used for pitched instruments to indicate that one note should be played smoothly into the next without a break (legato). Sometimes on string instruments this note is played as a slide.

Ties look similar to slurs but they rhythmically *join* two notes of equal pitch together.

Slurs do not occur in drum kit notation but it is helpful to know the difference.

Staccato

Staccato is a word for a very short note. You may at times see a dot over a note head. This indicates that the note is to be played 'staccato'.

In this example, you could catch the crash cymbal to shorten the sound.

Accents

Accents are widely used in drum notation and are represented by a '>'. Accents should be noticeably louder in volume than a regular stroke.

Double Bar-Lines

Double bar-lines show a change in the music. This may be a different time signature or merely another section in a long piece. They are used throughout this book at the end of each example. In this example, they are visible before a time signature change into **5/8**.

Repeat Signs

Repeat signs are a useful way to tell the performer to repeat the previous passages. When you encounter these symbols at the start and end of a section, you should repeat the part in between. Should you encounter *only* the 'end' repeat sign, then repeat everything from the start of the whole piece or the last double bar line.

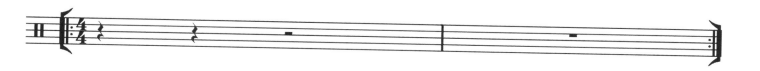

Simile Marks

Simile marks are repeat signs too. They save time when writing long pieces of music. You have encountered 1-bar repeat signs (%) in many examples up to now. The symbols below tell us to repeat the previous *two* bars.

Notice the extra line in the repeat symbol.

Volta Brackets

Volta brackets are written above the stave and show that a repeated passage has a different ending. The '1' is written above the notated first-time ending.

The notation above shows that we are to play through the piece and play the first ending as written. Then we need to repeat the passage and instead play the notated second ending (2). Volta brackets save writing out long identical parts with just a few notes different at the end.

Coda

The 'coda' (target) symbol is used in repeated passages to tell the performer when to skip to another sequence. This could be an ending for example. The piece might play through once, then repeat up until the coda, at which point playing is resumed at the *next* coda sign.

D.C.

'DC' is the symbol for 'Da Capo', literally meaning *from the beginning*.

'Da Capo *al fine*' tells the performer to repeat from the beginning to the end.

'Da Capo *al coda*' tells the performer to repeat from the beginning to the coda, then skip to the second coda.

Charts, Scores, Maps and Hits

Session drummers, both live and in the studio, are often given written musical notation to use as a guide. These guides are sometimes referred to by a number different names: *score*, *chart*, *road map*, or *the hits*, are just a few.

In certain situations, you will be required to play a drum pattern note for note. On other occasions, you might be given a basic drum part and asked to improvise around it. In other situations, like a jazz gig for example, you may only receive a chart with *the hits* written on.

Hits are usually written on one line or above the staff. Here is a typical example:

Notice how no specific drums are specified. All the drummer is given is the rhythm. There is an accent over the last 'hit'. This hit is to be played at a higher volume. On a drum kit this can be whatever orchestration you deem to be the most musical and appropriate.

Most drum charts contain a mixture of hits and written parts.

Let's now consolidate what you've learnt in this chapter into one piece of music!

Revision 3

Example 3t (80 Bpm)

Jazz swing on ride cymbal...

Revision 3 Guide

Bar 1-2: In 4/4. Repeat first 2 bars.

Bar 3-6: In 7/8. Play 1st time ending, then play bars 3,4,5 & **7** (second time ending).

Bar 10-11: Repeat previous 2 bars in 9/8 (represented by **two** lines in the repeat simile).

Bar 15: In 3/4. Rudimental notation. Closed roll is notated as 1/32nds (three lines on dotted 1/4 note)

Bar 16: bpm change to 180. Medium tempo swing. Swing each 1/8th note.

Bar 19: 1/8th note triplets notated over four 1/4 notes.

Bar 20-23: Jazz time on the ride cymbal. Improvisation here is at the player's discretion. Hits on bar 23 to be accentuated by the drummer.

Bar 24-27: Continue with the swing feel. Hits on bar 27 consisting of '1/4 note triplets' (Three 1/4 notes modified to fit the duration of beats 1 and 2).

Bar 32: Coda. Not played for now.

Bar 35: Repeat sign takes us back to bar 20. Play up to the coda.

Bar 32: This time we jump to the coda on bar 36 and play to the end of the piece.

How to Write Drum Parts by Hand

It is good practice to spend time writing out drum parts by hand. It's also a great way to remember any new ideas you might develop. Learning to write music helps with your reading speed and manuscript paper can be bought from most stationery stores or printed out at home from the internet.

Start with a blank staff:

Now add the relevant time signature:

Notating a simple 4/4 drum beat, we will start with the 1/4 note hi-hats. Split the bar evenly into four beats:

Next, we will 'fill in' a basic 1/8th note pattern:

(Don't worry if your first attempts are uneven and badly scrawled!)

Now, place the drum notes on the staff where you want them. Pay attention to where the notes should land in relation to the hi-hat part.

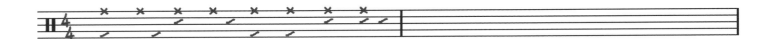

I have used simple pen strokes instead of full round note heads.

Now we add some basic tails to each note. Each tail should finish at roughly the same point above the stave.

Notice how the tails don't quite reach the note heads. When reading, you will find that you don't always need the tail to reach the note head, as in most printed notation.

Because I have used small strokes for the note heads, separating them from the tails makes each note more readily identified.

Next, by grouping the tails we can now notate the correct rhythm on each beat:

Be careful to write the note values correctly, including the adjoining 1/16th note tails.

Of course, this is not what a typical first attempt might look like, but with a familiarity and practice you can create neat and legible drum notation.

Writing out drum parts is not only convenient, it helps to keep your reading skills up to speed. You can use handwritten notation to make learning new songs easier. You don't even have to transcribe the whole drum part but may instead wish to make a note of stops, hits and important sections. Notes can be easily glanced at during performances as a quick reminder when necessary.

Well-honed reading and writing skills will stay with you forever so it pays to put in the hard graft now. Enjoy your newly acquired skill!

Conclusion

The key to quick and proficient reading is familiarity and practice. To improve your skills, it's important to spend time repeating exercises until they become second nature. Reading drum notation is no different than reading words from a page and in time it will become just as natural for you.

Groups of note heads will begin to take on the same significance as written words. It is the ability to recognise large chunks of rhythm in bite-size pieces that is the key to easily reading large passages of written music.

Take time with each exercise and pay close attention to the details; from stave line, to note head, to tail value. This, combined with physically playing the patterns on the drums, will set you on your way to becoming an accomplished reader and in-demand drummer.

Good luck, and have fun!

Kev

Further Reading

The following are some recommended books that develop rhythm, technique and drum notation. Some are written for snare drum only, and others are designed to accommodate drum kit players.

'Progressive Steps to Syncopation for the Modern Drummer' by Ted Reed

'The All-American Drummer' by Charley Wilcoxon

'The New Breed' by Gary Chester

'Advanced Funk Studies' by Rick Latham

'Master Studies' by Joe Morello

'Advanced Techniques for the Modern Drummer' by Jim Chapin

'Stick Control' by George Lawrence Stone

About the Author

With over 20 years' experience in the music industry, Kev O'Shea has been playing and educating throughout Ireland and worldwide. After studying Jazz in the renowned Newpark Music School of Dublin he has forged a successful career as an in-demand drummer, both live and in the studio.

With many years of extensive touring in Europe, America and the Middle East, Kev brings his expertise to his own website **www.KevOShea.com** where he provides lessons, tips & useful info for fellow drummers.

Other Books from Fundamental Changes

The Complete Guide to Playing Blues Guitar Book One: Rhythm Guitar

The Complete Guide to Playing Blues Guitar Book Two: Melodic Phrasing

The Complete Guide to Playing Blues Guitar Book Three: Beyond Pentatonics

The Complete Guide to Playing Blues Guitar Compilation

The CAGED System and 100 Licks for Blues Guitar

Fundamental Changes in Jazz Guitar: The Major ii V I

Minor ii V Mastery for Jazz Guitar

Jazz Blues Soloing for Guitar

Guitar Scales in Context

Guitar Chords in Context

Jazz Guitar Chord Mastery

Complete Technique for Modern Guitar

Funk Guitar Mastery

The Complete Technique, Theory and Scales Compilation for Guitar

Sight Reading Mastery for Guitar

Rock Guitar Un-CAGED: The CAGED System and 100 Licks for Rock Guitar

The Practical Guide to Modern Music Theory for Guitarists

Beginner's Guitar Lessons: The Essential Guide

Chord Tone Soloing for Jazz Guitar

Heavy Metal Rhythm Guitar

Heavy Metal Lead Guitar

Progressive Metal Guitar

Heavy Metal Guitar Bible

Exotic Pentatonic Soloing for Guitar

Voice Leading Jazz Guitar

The Complete Jazz Soloing Compilation

The Jazz Guitar Chords Compilation

Fingerstyle Blues Guitar

Printed in Great Britain
by Amazon